Men-at-Arms • 418

American Indians of the Pacific Northwest

Elizabeth von Aderkas • Illustrated by Christa Hook
Series editor Martin Windrow

First published in Great Britain in 2005 by Osprey Publishing,
Midland House, West Way, Botley, Oxford OX2 0PH, UK
44-02 23rd St, Suite 219, Long Island City, NY 11101, USA
Email: info@ospreypublishing.com

Osprey Publishing is part of the Osprey Group.

Transferred to digital print on demand 2009

First published 2005
1st impression 2005

Printed and bound by Cadmus Communications, USA

A CIP catalog record for this book is available from the British Library

ISBN: 978 1 84176 741 3

The right of Christa Hook to be identified as the illustrator of this work has been asserted in accordance
with ss77 and ss78 of the Copyright, Designs and Patents Act 1988.

Editorial by Martin Windrow
Design by Alan Hamp
Index by Glyn Sutcliffe
Origination by The Electronic Page Company

Dedication
This book is dedicated to the late Mrs June Wells

Acknowledgements
Special thanks to the staff of the Royal British Columbia Museum, Victoria, BC. Thanks also to the
Hudson Bay Archives, to Peter and Mable Knox, and to Patrick von Aderkas.

Artist's note
Readers may care to note that the original paintings from which the color plates in this book were prepared
are available for private sale. All reproduction copyright whatsoever is retained by the Publishers.
All enquiries should be addressed to:

Scorpio Gallery
PO Box 475
Hailsham
East Sussex
BN27 2SL
UK

The Publishers regret that they can enter into no correspondence upon this matter.

The Woodland Trust
Osprey Publishing is supporting the Woodland Trust, the UK's leading woodland conservation charity,
by funding the dedication of trees.

www.ospreypublishing.com

AMERICAN INDIANS OF THE PACIFIC NORTHWEST

INTRODUCTION

THE NORTHWEST was the last part of North America to be explored; contact between white men and Indians occurred only in 1774 on the Northwest Coast, and in 1805 on the Plateau. Those early explorers found a thriving aboriginal population, willing to trade with the newcomers. However, the lucrative fur trade, and a later series of gold discoveries, meant that the area rapidly became valuable to Europe and the United States. Settlers moved in and established their governments, and the native struggle for survival began.

Geographically, the Northwest stretches from southern Alaska down to northern California, and from the Pacific Ocean inland to the Rocky Mountains. This vast area contains two distinct native cultures: the Northwest Coast Indians and the Plateau Indians. The coastal natives live on a strip, no more than 150 miles wide, between the Pacific Ocean and the Cascade Mountains (the Canadian Coastal Mountains). The Plateau Indians live between the Cascades and the Rockies. The damp, abundantly fertile coast produced a very different culture from that which developed upon the arid Plateau. Nevertheless, the two groups shared a common history, and possibly some common roots.

The ancestors of the Northwest tribes are thought to have crossed the Bering land bridge from Siberia into Alaska at about 10,000 BC. The first human artifacts found on the coast date from roughly 8,000 to 9,000 BC. Excavations along the Columbia River show that the rich fishing spots close to the Dalles (see "Trade", below) have been inhabited for more than 10,000 years. One theory suggests that as the ice retreated after the last Ice Age, humans followed migrating game along a corridor east of the Rockies, and down to the area we now call the Plateau. From there, some of them traveled along the Kootenay and Columbia river systems, and reached the coast. The presence of Salishan people deep in the Plateau's interior as well as on the coast supports this theory.

Before the introduction of the horse at the beginning of the 18th century the two cultures were similar. The Spanish transported the horse to Mexico, and the Comanche traded it northwards. The densely forested coastal territory was impractical for horses; but the Plateau, with its rolling hills and grasslands, was perfectly suited, and the horse revolutionized Plateau life. Above all, it enabled hunting and raiding trips east of the Rockies, where young

Nootka man showing an example of a noble profile, with his forehead sloping back from the eyebrows. This was probably achieved through infantile head flattening. (Royal British Columbia Museum pn 4814)

braves had the opportunity to win honors and grow wealthy. The Plateau soon adopted Plains features, and culturally the Northwest Coast and Plateau grew further apart.

Neither culture had agriculture, but both survived adequately by fishing, hunting and gathering plants, berries and roots. The pursuit of food continued throughout the year on the Plateau, as the inhabitants moved around after seasonal supplies. Food sources on the Coast, however, were so abundant that several months' worth of food could be collected in a short time. The coastal peoples therefore had plenty of leisure to devote to culture and crafts.

Several historians have suggested that the Northwest Coast reached the apex of its culture after contact, when the tools, materials and fresh ideas brought by the whites encouraged a surge of creativity. In 1970 this theory was largely discredited by the discovery of Ozette in Washington State. Sometimes referred to as the "Pompei of North America", this archaeological site contained the well-preserved remains of several 500-year-old Makah longhouses, buried under a cliff. Ozette proved that life in the 16th century was just as rich and varied as in the 19th, and that the tribes already had access to iron, probably from Siberia.

The coastal culture displayed a rigid class system while the Plateau was relatively egalitarian. Both practiced slavery, but the coastal tribes went so far as to flatten their infants' heads to distinguish them from the slave class. There were similarities between the ceremonial lives of the two cultures, but the Coast had developed its rituals to a more elaborate level. Both peoples believed that a spirit guide determined the direction of an individual's life. On the Plateau, this was celebrated with a straightforward dance, in which an individual recounted his supernatural encounter. In some coastal tribes, however, these experiences were recounted in intricate ceremonies performed by exclusive dance societies, using "props", sound effects and stagecraft.

Traders brought guns to the Northwest, where they had an equally detrimental effect on both cultures, and spread rapidly through the area. In 1792 Captain George Vancouver was the first white man to reach Kwakiutl territory, but he found that the warriors had already obtained guns from the Nootka. Coastal intertribal wars had always been vicious, but fatalities rose dramatically once firearms were involved. From the Coast, guns were transported inland along the Fraser and Columbia river trade networks. The traditional conflict between the eastern Plateau tribes and the Blackfoot escalated in intensity once guns were introduced. The eastern tribes might have better withstood later waves of epidemics had they not been so drastically weakened in numbers by firearm warfare.

War was vital to both cultures. The people of the Northwest Coast were famously aggressive, especially the northern tribes of the Haida, Tlingit and Tsimshian and, further south, the Kwakiutl. Other coastal tribes such as the Salish made war to

Head flattening was practiced throughout the Coast. The infant's brow was flattened by pressure from cedar bark pads and wooden slats; this caused no brain damage, since the baby's skull bones were still relatively pliable and had not yet bonded rigidly. This painting of the late 1830s is by the great traveler and artist George Catlin. (Smithsonian American Art Museum, Gift of Mrs Joseph Harrison, Jr)

redress ancient feuds. Territorial boundaries on the Plateau shifted regularly; in ancient times this led to fighting as the tribes vied for the best hunting grounds. After the arrival of the horse, however, the Plateau tribes faced more major threats, since they were now vulnerable to attacks from the Plains and Great Basin Indians. Intertribal war in the region faded out, and the tribes joined alliances to fight their common enemies.

Infectious disease had wiped out all tribal warfare by the 1860s, but the Indians already faced another threat. From the 1840s onwards the US government tried to persuade the native population on to reservations. The resulting wars between the 1840s and 1870s formed part of the final American push to tame the West. Although they were eventually subdued, the Northwest tribes did not surrender quietly, and the story of their courageous if often hopeless wars makes fascinating reading.

TRIBES OF THE NORTHWEST COAST

The tribes of the Coast spoke over two dozen distinct languages. Each tribe was made up of isolated villages, every one an entity of its own. Although one tribe might enlist the help of a neighbor against a common enemy, they did not band together as they did on the Plateau. In spite of this independence, however, the groups shared many cultural traits: a rigid class structure, complex ceremonialism, and a high quality of craftsmanship.

Most of the anthropological information available today concentrates on the northern stretches of the coast. Little is known about the tribes south of the Columbia River; the area was settled so early that much of the evidence was destroyed. The northern tribes, however, still live in their original homelands in isolated regions of Alaska, northern British Columbia, and the outer coast of Vancouver Island. Furthermore, even though British and Canadian governments tried to ban native practices and ceremonies which they considered damaging, these continued in secret, and much of the original ritual is intact today.

Northern Coastal tribes:
Eyak, Tlingit, Tsimshian, Haida, Bella Coola, Haisla, Heiltsuk, Bella Bella, Ooweekeno and Kwakiutl

The Tlingit (pronounced *Klinkit*) lived in southeastern Alaska, where heavy rainfall produced a temperate climate. Another branch, known as the Inland Tlingit, lived in the southern Yukon, where conditions were more extreme. They were a warlike tribe, intent on expanding their territory; they absorbed lands belonging to the Eyak, their neighbors to the north, and periodically fought with the Tsimshian. When Russian fur traders moved on to the Coast in the late 18th century they met fierce resistance from the Tlingit. The tribes refused to trade with them, burned down trading posts and attacked Russian forts. Their aggression was a contributing factor to the Russian decision to withdraw from fur trading on the Coast, and eventually to sell Alaska to the Americans.

Tlingit, Haida and Tsimshian societies were organized into matrilineal clans. The names and number of clans varied from tribe to tribe, but usually included the raven, the eagle or the killer whale as their symbol. Children belonged to their mother's clan, and could only marry into their father's. Each clan owned a number of crests, and these were carved or painted on to every possession from fishing hooks to house posts. These matrilineal clans occurred throughout the Coast, but were most rigidly imposed among the three northernmost peoples.

The Tsimshian were powerful and wealthy. They lived on the Nass and Skeena rivers, both of which teemed with valuable eulachon fish in the spring (see "Fishing", below). Their neighbors, the Haida, were famous for their ocean-going canoes, which were up to 70 feet long and could carry some 30 warriors. Warfare was profitable, and the Haida raided for slaves and booty all the way down to California. Once the fur trade was established they made frequent trips to Fort Victoria; but in 1862 they brought smallpox back with them from one of these trips, which almost wiped out all of the northern tribes.

The Bella Coola lived on the Bella Coola River, some 75 miles from the sea. They spoke a form of Salishan, and had as elaborate a ceremonial life as the Tsimshian or the Kwakiutl. The Haisla, Heiltsuk, Bella Bella and Oowekeeno resembled the northern tribes, but were poorer; they also lived under constant threat from the Haida, since they were within convenient raiding distance of the latter. These tribes all spoke a form of Wakashan, a group of seven related languages found only on the Northwest Coast.

The Kwakiutl lived on northern Vancouver Island and the adjacent mainland of British Columbia. They were a forceful tribe, especially the Lekwiltok, who were feared all the way down to the Lower Columbia. They had guns by 1792, and pushed the Comox Salish out of Cape Mudge, a narrow strait through which all northerners had to pass to reach Fort Victoria. This gave the Lekwiltok an excellent ambush spot for canoe parties heading to the fort. The Kwakiutl had a highly developed ceremonial life that reflected their warlike nature. When intertribal warfare died out in the mid-19th century they modified the *potlatch*, a gift-giving ceremony, into a competitive and aggressive way to humiliate their enemies.

Central Coastal tribes:
Nootka, North Coast Salish, Central
Coast Salish and Makah

The name Nootka is a misnomer for Yuquot, inadvertently spread by British sailors. Captain Cook landed at Friendly Cove, Nootka Sound, in

1778, and was given otter pelts by the local natives. He then sold these skins in China for a huge profit, and the fur trade began. Nootka quickly became a trading port for Spaniards, Russians, Americans and British. Trade flourished all along the Coast until the 1840s, when the market declined. In 1802, Chief Maquinna of the Nootka took a ship's blacksmith, John Jewitt, as a slave and held him for two years. Jewitt escaped and wrote about his experience, giving us a clear account of life amongst the Nootka.

The North and Central Coast Salish were a collection of tribes speaking Salishan dialects. Their lands straddled what is now the border between Canada and the United States. The Makah lived on the Olympic Peninsula in Washington State, and were famous for whaling.

Southern Coastal tribes:
Southern Coast Salish, Kwalhioqua, Chinookans,
Clatskanie, Tillamook, Alseans, Kalapuyans,
Siuslawans, Coosans and Athapaskans

The Southern Coast Salish lived in Washington, and were made up of some 50 tribes who spoke two Salishan languages. They suffered at the hands of the Lekwiltok Kwakiutl, who mounted head-hunting raids into their territory, and several of the tribes joined forces to launch return attacks. They briefly fought the US in 1856, led by Chief Leschi of the Nisqually; but once defeated, they eventually settled into reservations.

The Chinookans lived at the mouth of the Columbia River, and came from the same language family as the Wasco Wishram on the Plateau side of the Cascades. These were a trading people who thrived during the fur trade. Foreign ships gave them muskets, shot and powder in exchange for tanned elk hides, which the white traders swapped for sea otter pelts further up the Coast. The Chinookans, in turn, traded the guns at the Dalles for vast profits.

Many of these Southern Coastal tribes led isolated lives before contact, and their numbers plummeted under the impact of successive smallpox epidemics. The Tillamook, described as plentiful by Lewis and Clark in 1805, were reduced to 200 people by the 1850s. Their descendants still live in Oregon, but are no longer officially recognized as a tribe. Only 29 Alseans and ten Siuslawans remained in 1910, all the surviving members merging with larger tribes.

The Kalapuyans of the Willamette Valley were hostile to white newcomers. They kept away from trading ships, and from Fort Astoria when it was built in 1811, but this isolation did not save them from disease. By the 1840s they were almost wiped out, and had lost too many of their number to put up any sort of resistance to the first white settlers of the Willamette Valley.

TRIBES OF THE PLATEAU

At the time of white contact some two dozen tribal groups lived on the Plateau. Most of these belonged to either the Sahaptin or the Salishan language families; the exceptions were the Athapaskans, Chinookans, Cayuse and Kootenai. The Salish occupied half the Plateau landmass, mostly the interior and north, with the Pend d'Oreille and Flathead in

the southeast. The Sahaptins lived along the Columbia River Basin, and as far south as northern California.

Tribes of the Salish country: Kootenai, Flathead, Pend d'Oreille, Shushwap, Lillooet, Thompson, Nicola, Okanagan, Lakes, Colville, Kalispel, Wenatchee, Chelan and Sanpoil

This section of the Plateau is the harshest and most inhospitable, and was inhabited by the hardiest of the tribes. The easternmost people – the Kootenai, Flathead and Pend d'Oreille – lived in the Rocky Mountains, hard against the Blackfoot, against whom they waged constant warfare. Consequently they were fierce warriors, and became natural allies of the equally warlike Nez Perce from the Columbia Basin. According to myth, the Kootenai had once lived east of the Rockies and were pushed west when the Blackfoot acquired horses. Certainly, these tribes lived under the shadow of the Plains, and had absorbed many of their cultural influences.

The northern Salish tribes – the Shushwap, Lillooet, Nicola and Thompson River – lived in the most inaccessible region of the Plateau, now the sparsely populated interior of British Columbia. These tribes were great hunters and traders. They remained isolated, however, and took little part in the large multi-tribal hunting and raiding parties that went to the Plains. In the 1860s gold miners tramped through the region on their way to the Cariboo gold rush in the north, but the area had few settlers to cause unrest. These tribes put up little resistance to the Canadian government, and settled on to reserves at the end of the 19th century.

To the south of the Thompson Indians, the bands of the Chelan, Sanpoil, and Wenatchee are often known as the Middle Columbia River Salish. Along with the Spokane, Colville, Okanagan, Lakes and Kalispel, they were part of a busy trade network linking the Plains with the Coast. The Kalispel lived at the entrance of the most accessible pass through the Rocky Mountains, and so benefited from eastern trade and traffic. These tribes had contacts with the Columbia Basin tribes, and joined in the composite raiding and bison hunting expeditions to the Plains. They also traded at the Dalles, and joined in the 1856 and 1858 Yakima wars against the US authorities.

The Columbia River tribes: Nez Perce, Coeur d'Alene, Cayuse, Umatilla, Walla Walla, Palouse, Warm Springs/Tenino, Yakima and Wasco Wishram

The southern tribes of the Plateau lived along the Columbia River and its tributaries. Apart from the Wasco Wishram and the Cayuse, most spoke dialects of Sahaptin language stock. The area was dominated by the Nez Perce, who lived in territory stretching across the modern state lines of Washington, Oregon and Idaho. They waged war against the Shoshone to the south and the Blackfoot to the east. Said to be the best horsemen on the Plateau, they were also highly skilled with the bow and arrow, and later with the gun.

When they reached marriageable age high-ranking women from the three northernmost tribes began to wear a labret, an elliptical wooden plug inserted through a slit in the lower lip. A young woman would start with a small plug, which increased in size with her age and wealth; a prosperous, elderly woman could end up with a labret 3in long. This engraving made in 1787 shows a Haida woman from the Queen Charlotte Islands. (University of Washington Libraries, Special Collections NA 3938)

The Walla Walla and the Umatilla lived on the Columbia and Walla Walla rivers, and were closely allied with the Nez Perce through marriage and trade. The Cayuse lived in the Blue Mountains; their population declined during a long-running war with the Snake Indians to the south. By 1851 there were few pure-blood Cayuse left, and they had been absorbed into the Nez Perce. Gradually, Nez Perce became the language of trade among these tribes.

The Warm Springs Indians were also known as the Tenino, and were closely connected with their neighbors the Walla Walla. They acted as scouts for the US Army in the Modoc War of the 1870s. The Yakima occupied territory to the north, and had close connections with the Northwest Coast, particularly the Coastal Salish. The Wasco Wishram lived along the Columbia River, and the Dalles, the most important trading rendezvous on the Plateau, lay in their territory. Here the Columbia River narrowed to form the first major portage for canoes paddling in from the Coast. Tribes came to fish, gamble and trade. The Nez Perce and the Cayuse kept well-armed parties permanently camped at the Dalles, hoping to corner the largest possible share of guns and knives passing inland from the Coast.

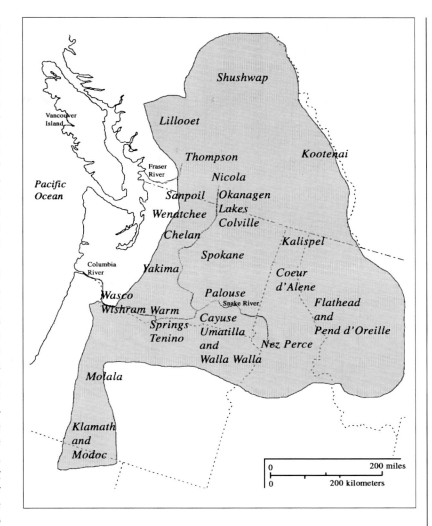

Map of the Plateau, showing modern state and international boundaries.

The Southern tribes: Molala, Klamath and Modoc

These tribes lived on the eastern slopes of the Cascade Mountains, down through Oregon and into northern California. They were completely isolated from their neighbors until the Hudson's Bay Company persuaded them out of seclusion to trap for pelts. The Klamath and Modoc could be classified as Great Basin tribes, but their languages were connected to the Sahaptin family. In the first part of the 19th century they began slave trading at the Dalles, where they mixed with other Plateau tribes and absorbed their characteristics. The Klamath and Modoc were closely related but were mutually antagonistic. In the 1860s the authorities put them both on the same reservation, which was to be one of several causes of the later Modoc War.

9

In 1862, lay minister William Duncan founded the model village of Metlakatla with 50 Tsimshian followers. Native interest in the project was lukewarm until the smallpox epidemic of that year devastated Port Simpson but left Metlakatla relatively untouched; hundreds more Indians then joined the village. Duncan eventually fell out with the Anglican Church, and moved the entire village to Alaska. Photograph by Edward Dossetter. (British Columbia Archives B-03573)

CHRONOLOGY

1700	Horses first arrive on the Plateau.
1774	First contact on the Coast. Juan Josef Pérez Hernández sails to the 55th Parallel, and meets a party of Haida off the Queen Charlotte Islands.
1778	Captain James Cook lands at Nootka Sound. The fur trade begins.
1780s–90s	Smallpox outbreaks on the southern Coast.
1792	Captain George Vancouver sails up the Northwest Coast.
1793	Fur trader Alexander Mackenzie crosses the Rocky Mountains, and travels through the northern interior of today's British Columbia to Bella Coola territory on the Coast.
1805–06	Meriwether Lewis and William Clark are the first white men to reach the Plateau, and travel along the Columbia River to the Northwest Coast. Trade expeditions follow.
1821	The merger of the Hudson's Bay Company and the Northwest Company.
1840s	Decline in fur prices leads to the end of the fur trade. Settlers start up the Oregon Trail.
1846	Boundary drawn between the United States and Canada along the 49th Parallel.
1847	Outbreak of measles among the Cayuse; Cayuse War.
1855	Treaty-making begins in the United States between the government and the tribes of the Columbia Plateau; the Walla Walla Council.
1855–56	Yakima War, involving the Yakima, Walla Walla, Umatilla and Cayuse.
1858	Coeur d'Alene War in Washington Territory, involving the Coeur d'Alene, Spokane, Palouse, Yakima, Walla Walla, Umatilla and Northern Paiute.
1861–65	American Civil War.
1862	Severe smallpox epidemic ravages Northern Coastal tribes.
1867	Confederation of Canada.

1869	US Union Pacific railroad completed; more settlers pour in.
1872–73	Modoc War in California and Oregon.
1877	Flight of the Nez Perce.
1884	Canadian Indian Act outlaws the potlatch and winter ceremonies.

CLOTHING, HOUSING AND CANOES

Clothing on the Coast

In summer men wore as little as possible, and in winter only a robe made from shredded cedar bark. Women wore an apron and skirt of the same material. Both sexes added a short shoulder-length cape for extra warmth; these were trimmed with fur to stop the rough bark chafing against the skin. Rain was a fact of life on the Coast, and women constructed poncho-like raincoats out of cedar matting; wide-brimmed hats were made of tightly woven basketwork. Moccasins were seldom worn, since they fell apart quickly in the rain, but some tribes sewed them out of salmon skin.

The northern stretches of the Coast were temperate, and the Tlingit and the Eyak wore the same woven bark clothing as the southern tribes. They had garments for the extreme cold of hunting trips to the interior, usually a fur tunic and a set of thick hide trousers with moccasins attached. Few coastal Indians wore hide clothing; it was more common south of the

Flathead chief and child. Their ceremonial clothing shows strong Plains influence, especially the feather headdress, the long breechcloth, and the beaded buckskin moccasins. Ceremonial wear was determined by rank, and by instructions received from the individual's guardian spirit in visions. (Denver Public Library, Western History Collection, Edward Boos BS4)

The cedar provided many of the material needs of the Coast peoples. This man using a hand fire-drill was photographed at Koskimo in northern Vancouver Island. His clothing is characteristically made from the soft inner layer of cedar bark that had been "begged" from the tree, beaten into strands and woven together into garments. (British Columbia Archives D-08296)

Columbia River, suggesting that the Chinookans brought the skins in from the Dalles and traded them with the Southern Coastal tribes.

Hair was worn long and braided. All infants, except those born to slaves, had their heads flattened. Hats were made of basketwork; Nootka chiefs wore cone-shaped hats with a pointed ball on the top and whaling scenes woven into the sides.

The tribes of the Coast freely decorated their faces, bodies and clothes. The type of ornamentation depended on their rank, and the demands of each day or occasion. Everyday face paint was a mixture of grease and coloring to prevent sunburn. More elaborate painting was applied for warfare, at feasts and on whaling expeditions.

High-ranking Tlingit, Tsimshian and Haida women wore a labret – an elliptical wooden plug – through a slit in the lower lip. Strands of dentalia shell were worn as necklaces or earrings, or pierced singly through the nasal septum. Once fur-trading ships arrived, the Indians made bracelets and neck rings out of trade metal and copper. These northern tribes also tattooed matrilineal crests on their arms and chests. Further south, the women of the Lower Columbia restricted tattooing to three small vertical lines on the chin. The Lower Columbia men had a measurement tattooed on their arms that allowed them to measure the length of a dentalium shell.

Clothing on the Plateau

Before the coming of the horse, both men and women wore fringed skirts, capes and leggings woven from shredded plant fibers, similar to the cedar bark garments of the Coast. In summer men wore nothing at all, but the women were always modestly covered with woven robes. In winter they wore woven moccasins lined with sage bark, and added fur robes to their bark clothing – often of fox or wolf, but the wealthy would wear robes of bear or elk skins.

After the arrival of the horse the Plateau came under Plains influence and most clothing was made of deer hide. Hunting methods changed with the introduction of the horse, allowing large numbers of deer to be trapped at once. By the mid-19th century even the most isolated tribes on the Plateau wore Plains-style clothing. Men now wore hide leggings, moccasins and shirts, all of which were beaded and fringed for ceremonial occasions. Women wore beaded deerskin dresses down to mid-calf, tied with a wide belt, and short hide leggings from knee to ankle.

Buckskin was extremely practical for Plateau life, being tough, long-lasting and warm. The women cured the skins and made them supple; some tribes softened the hides in a solution of deer brains to achieve the right degree of pliability. The Salish favored white clothing, and would bleach the hide by rubbing in white clay.

Horses made the hunting of big game easier, and the large composite bison-hunting expeditions to the Plains brought home a steady supply

Haida raven totem displaying the crest figures of the household; such totems could be up to 50 feet high. The photograph shows a modern entrance cut into the wall, but the original entrance would have been through an opening in the bottom figure of the pole. (British Columbia Archives H-07207)

of "buffalo" skins. These large skins were scraped, tanned and stretched by women at the Plains hunting camp.

Women along the Columbia Basin wore twined basketwork hats made from either bark or tule (bulrush). Men wore a simple headband with an eagle feather. As Plains influence increased, chiefs adopted feathered headdresses – either the simple standing circlet of eagle feathers (see picture of Flathead chief on page 11), or the more elaborate "trailer" bonnet with a long rear train.

Clothing was extensively decorated. Before contact, the tribes favored dentalia shell, bone, bear claws, feathers and porcupine quills. Designs were often painted or scorched on to buckskin garments. Holes were punched to show immunity from weapon wounds. After contact, the fur companies introduced traded beads. At first these were large blue so-called Murano beads; then "pony beads", about the size of a corn kernel; and finally the tiny "seed beads" that became so popular in Plains and Plateau clothing. The Columbia Basin tribes developed their own beading style, especially noted among the Nez Perce and Cayuse. They combined this with their love of horses to produce finely beaded horse paraphernalia such as harnesses and hoods.

Hair was worn long; only slaves and people in mourning wore it cut short, and adulterers had one side of their hair sheared off. The men of the Columbia River tribes had the front fringe cut short and swept up into a pompador. Women combed their men's hair, parted and plaited it. Salmon oil was rubbed in to make it shine.

Housing on the Coast

The most common house style was the rectangular cedar-frame structure. The roof beams and corner posts were permanently in place, but the walls and roofing were made of removable planks. The village could move from the winter to the summer site, taking the wall and roof planks with them. Two canoes were lashed side by side and the house planks laid across them, thus creating a stable platform on which to transport the piled-up household goods.

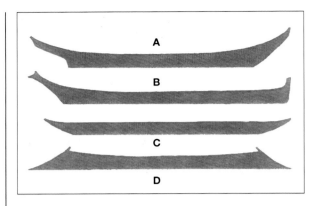

Silhouettes of characteristic canoes – not to scale. The prow is to the left in each case:
(A) A Northern Coast canoe with fine lines, and high projections at prow and stern.
(B) The West Coast style canoe carried a prow extension in the form of an alert animal.
(C) The Plateau dug-out was much simpler than the ocean-going canoes, but stable and sturdy on lakes and rivers.
(D) Plateau Kootenai bark canoe; the inner framework was of wood, covered with birch bark. Light and easily portaged, these could nevertheless carry heavy cargoes. The sturgeon-nose shape allowed them to pass through shallows, and kept water out when negotiating rapids.

These houses held several families. The walls were usually painted with family crests, and totem poles stood against the front facade. Inside there was a central fire pit, but each family would have a separate cooking fire of its own. Dried fish and meat hung down from hooks on the ceiling, and the walls were stacked with finely carved cedar storage boxes. Sweat houses were much simpler structures than on the Plateau. They were put up, as needed, using whatever was at hand – usually branches covered with matting.

Occasionally, coastal tribes dug pit houses for purposes of defense, or in extreme cold. Only the roof of the house was visible, and this could be camouflaged from the enemy with branches and leaves.

Housing on the Plateau

Before the arrival of the horse, tribes lived in winter villages on the banks of rivers. In summer these groups split up into smaller camps to search out different seasonal foods. For gathering spring roots and summer berries they camped in the mountains; other groups headed to the rivers for salmon runs, or to the hills for hunting. The winter homes were semi-permanent, but summer lodging had to be transportable. The pit houses used in winter villages were excavated 3–4ft underground, the roofs being covered with branches, woven mats and grasses; they were warm, solid and secure, and the grass roofs served as effective camouflage. Four or five families lived in a house, for a total of up to about 30 people.

Summer lodges had log frames, with sides of matting or planks, and a wooden roof. Once horses arrived the villages no longer clung to the riverbanks, seeking out instead the best grasslands for the herds. Many tribes adopted the Plains tepee; made with buffalo skins, these were light, warm, waterproof, and took very few people to construct or move. As the Plateau population dwindled due to disease, this became an important consideration.

In addition to the houses, villages had other structures for any activity that required seclusion. Amongst these were the childbirth lodge, the girls' puberty lodge, the sweat lodge, and pit houses for dried food.

Canoes

The canoe was common to both cultures. Before the horse, the Plateau river networks were the main highways for trade and war. The canoe lost some importance with the adoption of the horse but still played an important role in daily life. It was always central to life on the Coast; there were no trails between villages, so the sea was the only way to travel. Babies were sometimes put in canoe-shaped cradleboards, and the dead laid to rest in old canoes resting on scaffolding.

Haida canoes were the most admired. These dug-outs were fast, well adapted to the rough offshore waters. Their traditional large raised prows were designed to display the chief's crests, as well as to provide some protection from enemy arrows as they landed. The Tlingit treasured Haida canoes, covering them in their own crests, giving them names, and strengthening the prows so that they could break through ice. At the other end of the scale, the West Coast style canoe was useful rather than sleek. Built for convenience rather than speed, it was ideal for transporting passengers, household items and trade goods. This made it a sought-after trade item itself, up and down the Coast and even among the Wasco Wishram.

There were two types of canoe on the Plateau, the bark and the dug-out. The bark canoe was usually made of birch, and was light, versatile and ideal for travel on lakes. Usually made out of Ponderosa pine, cottonwood or cedar, the dug-out was less common. With the introduction of iron tools, however, it became easier to make. A log was hollowed out by fire until the walls were thin, but would keep the trunk's original outer contour. On the Northwest Coast canoes were produced in much the same way, but their craftsmen were highly skilled at using controlled burning techniques. The carvers lit one side of the log, and when it was cool scraped out the charred pieces with knives made of shell. They gradually enlarged the cavity until it was the right shape, then rolled the log over and shaped the keel in the same way.

HUNTING, FISHING & TRADE

Hunting on the Plateau

Life on the Plateau was dominated by the need to find food. Hunting was the most important activity, and the skills needed were almost as highly valued as prowess in war. Warriors could excuse themselves from a war party if they had hunting duties. Skillful hunters were believed to be blessed by an especially powerful guardian spirit.

Throughout the year the tribes moved around after the best game. Deer was the most important catch, for its hide as well as its meat. Elk was also prized, for meat and for the skins, which were used as robes and bedding, and for the teeth, which were sewn on to ceremonial garments as decoration. Mountain goats provided wool and meat and their horns were used as drinking cups. Grizzly bears were killed for their skins rather than their meat, which was too strongly flavored. Killing a grizzly was a brave act, and enhanced the hunter's reputation. They used poisoned arrows, or special long spears that allowed the hunter to impale the bear while staying out of range of its powerful front legs and huge claws.

A Coeur d'Alene man and a small boy on horseback bring home a deer from the hunt; note the dog, and the puppy riding behind the boy. Deer hunting took place in spring and mid-winter; the average family needed 20 to 40 deer per year for food and clothing. (Northwest Museum of Arts and Culture/ Eastern Washington State Historical Society, Spokane, Washington, L95-109.120)

Before the introduction of the horse, hunting needed a great deal of manpower. Even the simplest method needed several hunters to encircle the herd and shoot into it with bows and arrows. However, the Indians also drove herds over cliffs, at the bottom of which hunters waited to finish off the injured animals. Dogs were used for herding, or undergrowth was set on fire to panic the animals in a certain direction. The introduction of the gun was a mixed blessing: any advantages gained by firepower were off-set by the noise, which frightened the other animals, and made the prey species increasingly shy of humans. Furthermore, the traditional encircling tactics might lead to gun-armed hunters killing each other in the crossfire.

After the introduction of the horse the Plateau tribes began to hunt buffalo east of the Rockies in composite tribal parties. These usually included a selection of the young and the healthy from the Flatheads, Pend d'Oreille, Spokane, Kootenai and Nez Perce. These were major expeditions, which faced hardship and danger; they could involve up to 1,000 men, and might last three years. The journey to the Plains took weeks, and was undertaken in the spring when most of the rivers were in full flood. The party faced uncertain hunting conditions and hostile tribes, especially the Piegan Blackfoot. Nevertheless, such expeditions could be highly advantageous to a young man. Any deed of bravery in the hunt was rewarded with high honors; and since a buffalo skin belonged to the man who had made the kill, brave and skillful hunters also went home wealthy.

Every party had a hunt leader who organized the expedition like a military campaign. He ensured that all the ceremonial preparations were properly executed, and that weapons were made ready. He judged conditions, planned strategies, and coordinated the hunters. Afterwards, he made sure that meat and skins were properly preserved by the women in the camp, and that the entire kill was fairly divided.

Hunting, like most serious activities, was inseparable from the Plateau's religious life. As such, it mixed practical considerations with ceremonial. For example, before an important expedition hunters would purify themselves with sessions in the sweat lodge, followed by a plunge in an icy lake. Spiritually, they aimed to cleanse their souls, but physically, they wanted to rid themselves of as much human odor as possible, in order to creep up on the game. They sang and prayed continuously. The hunted animal was to be respected and honored, both before and after a kill. Once the animal was dead they prayed to it, and butchered it in a ritualistic manner, giving thanks as they did so.

The Makah and Nootka were renowned whalers (see also Plate D1). Typically, a crew of six men harpooned a whale from a canoe. They killed it with short daggers, wrapped a line with sealskin floats – see right – around its neck to stop it sinking, and dragged it to shore. Photograph by Edward S.Curtis. (Royal British Columbia Museum pn 4984)

Fishing on the Plateau

Five varieties of salmon swam in the rivers of the Plateau, along with trout, steelhead and sturgeon. Fishing methods involved trapping as many fish as possible. To this end the Indians constructed large communal weirs out of wickerwork, which would trap the fish while

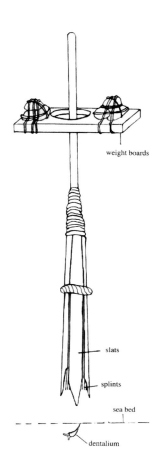

weight boards

slats

splints

sea bed

dentalium

ABOVE **The dentalium is a marine invertebrate with a hard white shell of a tapering, slightly curved horn shape. Greatly prized for decorative purposes and thus commanding a high value in trade, dentalia formed an important part of the Nootka economy. They were usually found in very deep sea beds, but due to a freak convergence of currents they also grew in accessible (but secret) beds just off Vancouver Island. The dentalia were gathered by using this ingenious device. Nootka harvesters stood in a canoe above the dentalia beds and lowered the broom-like contraption to the sea floor; sections were added to the handle until it reached up to 70ft in length. The weight board was then lowered, sinking slowly down over the head, and thus forcing the outer slats closed and pinching the inner splints together, trapping the dentalia. The harvest was then pulled to the surface.**

letting the water flow through. The catch was then divided up amongst the village. Several tribes specialized in constructing funnel-shaped traps that allowed the fish to swim in but not out. Some fishing spots were used by several tribes at once. These usually occurred where the rivers narrowed, or at waterfalls, where large numbers of fish would be forced through small gaps. The different tribes camped together at these places, where they constructed communal wooden platforms from which they fished with spears or dip nets. Fish had to be preserved for later use or trade. Mostly it was smoked or dried, and many tribes pounded the dried salmon flesh to produce a flour. This was packed into hide bags, and traded.

Hunting and fishing on the Coast

There was abundant game on the Coast, but the terrain was so rugged and thickly wooded that the tribes did not often hunt it – sea mammals provided a more readily available source of meat. Seals and sea lions were dispatched with clubs, as the animals were slow and clumsy when they climbed on to the rocks. Harpoons and bows and arrows were used to kill sea otters, porpoises and whales.

Salmon were even more plentiful on the Coast than the Plateau, and could be caught in large numbers as they returned to fresh water to spawn and die. The advantage of salmon was that it was so quick and easy to preserve that a family could catch and dry several months' worth of food in just a few days. The traps were as intricate as on the Plateau, often woven out of red cedar bark. In addition to salmon the coastal tribes ate herring, and sea food such as crabs, clams and mussels were available for most of the year.

The eulachon fish was found only on Tsimshian and Kwakiutl territory, but was essential to the diet of the entire Coast. It was also called the Candle Fish, as it was so impregnated with oil that it could be lit like a candle. The Tsimshian dried some of the catch, but used most of it to make oil. Canoes full of fresh eulachon were tipped into pits and buried for a short while to let them rot slightly. This made them easier to render and, according to coastal tradition, added a richer taste to the oil. The semi-putrid fish were then boiled in water and the oil skimmed off. The coastal natives poured it over all food, including summer berries. Possibly, it compensated for the fact that there was very little starch in the coastal diet.

Oil also came from whales. The Nootka and Makah were the most famous whalers; they hunted from large canoes crewed by several men, with harpoons, lances, and large buoys made from seal bladders.

Dentalia were harvested from the sea and formed a very important part of the Nootka tribal economy. Dentalia were sold strung, about 40 together in lengths of one fathom; the larger the shells, the more valuable they were, but a fathom typically bought one male or two female slaves.

Trade on the Plateau

Wealth meant owning tradable goods; the value of these goods depended on the labor it took to produce them and the price paid for them. Traditional trading routes lay along the river systems, and aboriginal trading posts grew up at fishing spots. Examples are Kettle Falls in Colville territory, the Celilo Falls on the Columbia River, and, most famous of all, the Dalles in Wasco Wishram country.

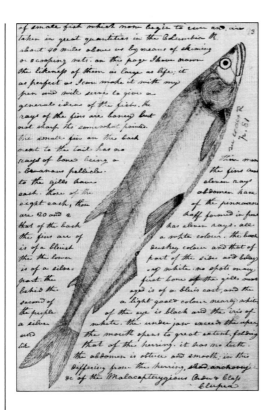

Eulachon – a drawing from the *Journals* of Lewis and Clark. When their party spent the spring of 1806 at the mouth of the Columbia River the Chinookans brought them eulachon, and Meriwether Lewis described the fish as "lussious" (sic). Apart from being a food source, it was rendered to provide an oil which was used throughout the Coast and was an important trade resource for the Tsimshian people. (American Philosophical Society. Lewis and Clark J93)

This Haida carved "grease" dish shows the crest figures of a sealion and a thunderbird. This beautifully carved piece shows the respect the coastal people had for eulachon oil. (Royal British Columbia Museum cn 410)

The Dalles was where the Plateau met the Northwest Coast. By the late 18th century European goods were pouring on to the Coast with the early fur trade, and the tribes of the Plateau had their first taste of these treasures at the Dalles. In the same period a party of Cayuse and Walla Walla chiefs went to California and opened a trading route for horses and cattle. They brought back trade items from California which were redistributed through the region via the Dalles.

Soon after contact with the white man, guns made their way to the Dalles. This led to a continual Nez Perce and Cayuse presence there, whose determination to secure a large share of these benefits led to bullying and fights with the more peaceful traders. The Dalles, however, was more than a trading place. Gambling and horseracing were popular pastimes. Many intertribal marriages were arranged; new ideas and religions were spread (and so, unfortunately, were the new diseases).

There was no single form of currency at the Dalles, but Nootka dentalia was widely used. It was so popular that the Hudson's Bay Company tried to introduce a synthetic version, which was immediately detected by the Indians. Horses became the most desirable trade item, and this stimulated the slave trade. Many tribes, such as the Modoc, were poor, with few tradable goods; as soon as they realized that slaves could buy horses, they became fierce raiders of the Californian tribes such as the Shasta.

The fur trade upset the old tribal order on the Plateau. The Hudson's Bay Company and Northwest Company paid many Indians to work as trappers, and these then became the "middle men" between their own tribes and the white fur traders. This made them wealthier and more powerful than the chiefs, and caused tension in the tribes.

"Chinook" jargon was used for trade. This is not to be confused with the Upper Chinook dialect of the Chinookan people; it was a pidgin language that used a mixture of native and European languages and hand signals. It was widespread, up and down the Coast as well as on the Plateau. The tribes used it into the late 19th century, when English took over as the universal language. As trade changed, the language evolved with it. An essentially primitive mixture of language and signing, Chinook nevertheless served its purpose for trading relations; but it met its limits when used by white government in the treaty-making process and in law courts. For these purposes it was quite inadequate, and left the native parties to these exchanges ignorant about all but the most obvious points, to their disadvantage.

Trade on the Coast

Traditional trade ran up and down the Coast. The Tlingit traded walrus ivory and hides for Haida canoes. The West Coast style canoe, made by the Salish, was traded widely, since it was a versatile, practical vessel. Animal pelts such as beaver and sea otter were also valuable long before contact and trade with the white man. Such durable objects were seldom traded, but kept as insurance against emergencies or famine.

This 1853 engraving of the Dalles by J.M.Stanley is a peaceful depiction of one of the most intensely fished stretches of the Columbia River. The site of a year-round trading village, it was an important meeting point between the Coast and Plateau peoples. (University of Washington Libraries, Special Collections NA 4170)

The eulachon fish was vital to the Tsmishian economy. Every spring a huge trading camp was set up at the mouth of the Nass River. When the trading forts were constructed on the Coast, the Hudson's Bay Company built them on the original "grease trail" that connected the tribes with the source of Tsimshian eulachon. Even the Tsimshians' traditional rivals the Tlingit were forced to bury the hatchet long enough to negotiate the year's supply of eulachon oil. The peace was fragile, however, and fights often erupted at the Nass River camp.

The fur trade brought little change on the Coast itself, but it meant access to guns, wealth and increased trade with the Plateau tribes, who wanted a share of the new European goods. Increased trade led to closer relations between the two cultures. The Tlingit were possessive about their trade routes to interior tribes; they destroyed a Hudson's Bay Company trading post rather than let the white traders anywhere near their patch.

RELIGION AND CEREMONIAL LIFE

Since the spiritual life of the Northwest Indians is inseparable from their secular life, this section will touch on all the other sections, especially hunting, fishing and war.

Ceremonial life on the Plateau

The natives of the Plateau respected all of nature, and believed everything living or inanimate had a soul. According to their myths, the world was once full of spirits in human form. Each spirit had a particular power which it passed on to a specially chosen human; the spirit became that person's guide. This supernatural contact would determine the child's occupation and direction in life.

Boys, and sometimes girls, were sent off on a vision quest when they reached puberty. This was a time of transition to both the adult and the spiritual world. They went off alone to a well-known sacred place, and through starvation, thirst and cold, tried to fall into a trance. They remained

Two men from the Flathead Reservation sit beside a sweat lodge made by laying blankets over a framework of sticks. Hot rocks from the fire were placed inside the metal bucket visible beside the entrance. Once inside the lodge, water was splashed on the rocks to produce steam. (Denver Public Library, Western History Collection. Edward Boos BS43)

in this state until a spirit spoke to them. If nothing happened, they went back to the sweat lodge, purified themselves, and set out again.

Most Plateau tribes held a Winter Spirit Dance. These varied from tribe to tribe, but usually involved a performer dramatizing his encounter with a spirit guide. He sang songs learned on his original quest, but relearned now he had had time to grow into his acquired power and abilities.

Shamans were initiated during the Winter Spirit Dance. They became shamans by going on the same spirit quest as their contemporaries, but not all spirits were equal, and the shamans were chosen by the more powerful, such as the Sweat Lodge Spirit. Shamans presided over the tribe's spiritual life, and were used for curing, cursing, exorcising evil spirits and retrieving lost souls. In certain ceremonies the villagers sang and asked the spirits questions, and the spirits screamed their responses through the shaman.

The Sweat Lodge Spirit was powerful because the sweat lodge was fundamental to ceremonial life; the Kalispel even called this spirit "Grandfather". Sweating cured both physical and spiritual illness, granting protection from evil and imparting strength and good luck. The villagers would visit the sweat lodge before war, hunting or gambling; most sessions in the lodge were followed by a plunge in a lake or river. After contact with the white man, however, sweat lodge cures only helped to hasten the spread of infectious disease.

All the tribes celebrated first foods, whether salmon, berries or roots. The principle was the same: the food had to be treated with respect. The first salmon caught each season was killed in a special way, its flesh was portioned out amongst the tribe and the bones returned to the river. The first basket of berries picked or roots dug were shared out in a similar way. Other Plateau ceremonies were borrowed from neighbors: the Kootenai and the Nez Perce, for instance, had adopted forms of the Sun Dance from the Plains tribes, and the Yakima, Shushwap and Lillooet all had variations on the coastal *potlatch* (see below).

War dances were common to most tribes and were usually held before an engagement to rally the warriors and encourage a bellicose mood. These dances functioned as a warm-up for the real fight, as the warriors often staged mock battles or practiced dodging arrows. After the battle, if the tribe returned to their village victorious, they held a Scalp Dance (see below, "Warfare").

New native religions grew up after 1800. The fur trade on the Coast, and the arrival of whites along the Columbia and Fraser rivers, brought rapid change. On the Plateau the Washat or Dreamer Religion quickly caught on, being spread through contacts at the Dalles. Washat was introduced by Smohalla, a Wanapum Indian from

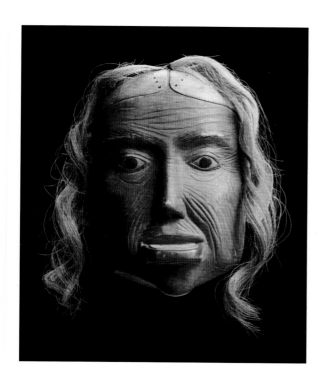

Haida dance society mask of the character "Old Woman", complete with labret. After the arrival of missionaries Haida winter dances died out, but from the 1840s onwards there was a demand for dance masks and argillite carvings from sailors and traders, thus creating the Coast's first tourist industry. (Canadian Museum of Civilization VII-B-6, image no.S92-4162)

OPPOSITE At the Chicago World Fair, 1893, a Kwakiutl performer demonstrates the War Dance. During the winter ceremonials the dancer was so imbued with warrior spirit that the other dancers tied him into a harness and hoisted him up to the roof beams, to allow the tribe a period of peace. Once in position, the dancer would pierce his skin to demonstrate his bravery and resistance to pain. Photograph by Charles Carpenter. (The Field Museum, CSA 13594)

the Columbia River. As a young man, he left the region and walked through California and Mexico, later claiming to have been to the spirit world. He predicted the future through visions, urging his followers to reject all white influence and return to traditional ways. Smohalla had many Nez Perce followers, and his teachings would encourage them to rebel against the US government's reservation restrictions in 1877.

Ceremonial life on the Coast

The coastal tribes had a ceremonial season in winter, and believed that the spirits were closer during that time of year. The Coast Salish had their version of the Plateau's Winter Spirit Dance; the ceremony involved several nights of dancing, and each dancer would sing about his supernatural experience. Other Northwest Coast tribes had a more elaborate version of the story, which involved not just an encounter, but also the spirit abducting the human to the Upper World. The dancer would then act out his return to the village in a wild and violent state, and show off his newly acquired powers. The rest of the tribe would have to tame him with songs and dances. This basic story could be told in an infinite number of ways.

The ceremonial life of Coast society reflected its intricate class system. Ceremonies were not open to everyone. The Bella Coola had two dancing societies, the Sisaok and the Kusiut, and these only admitted members from high-ranking families. Both societies performed dances telling of supernatural encounters, but Sisoak dances recounted their ancestors' exploits in the spirit world. This allowed each dancer to display his family crests and finery, and to sing songs about his ancestors' noble past.

The Kusiut dances were based on the supernatural abduction theme, with the difference that they tried to make non-members watching the dance believe that the spirits were actually in the room with them. The dancers usually performed in a dark hall, in front of one central fire. In this dim lighting they used theatrical tricks and sound effects to deceive the crowd: wooden whistles were hidden under blankets, and goat's bladder bellows were squeezed under someone's armpit. A couple of members of the society were stationed on the roof to thump out the arrival of the spirit. Elaborate mechanical masks showed transformations of one creature to another. These masks were ordered specifically for each dance, then burnt afterwards. Secrecy was fundamental to the Kusiut. The dances could be terrifying, which helped keep the audience at a respectful distance. The Cannibal Dance was particularly horrifying, as the untamed cannibal ran around the room biting the audience. The society had marshals who made sure that no one leaked secrets to the non-initiated. They recruited spies to check on any villagers showing signs of skepticism, or any of their members suspected of disclosing secrets – and the penalty for betrayal was death.

The Kwakiutl had a similarly elaborate set of winter dances. All performers were called shamans for the duration of the season. They also performed the Cannibal Dance, but had many other performances that demonstrated how various characters acquired supernatural power. The Warrior Woman, for example, asked to have her head cut off after the Warrior Spirit had abducted her and sent her home mad. The Warrior Spirit also abducted the Warrior Dancer, and left him so addicted to war that when he returned to the village his friends had to string him up from the ceiling in order for the tribe to have a rest from fighting.

The Potlatch

The word comes from Chinook, meaning "to give". The potlatch was held to establish social position, and to make official any important change in tribal life. For example, when a man inherited his father's position as chief he did not acquire this status until the potlatch had been held. Guests were invited to witness his assumption of the new title, and they were paid for their participation with gifts and a feast.

The ceremony involved not just the host, but his entire extended family, who all contributed goods. At the end of the ceremony the whole family would be bankrupt, but they would receive everything back with interest when their guests hosted their own potlatches. Giving and receiving evened out, and the system kept wealth circulating. The ceremony was so fundamental to the culture that children in many tribes hosted play potlatches so that they could learn the protocol.

The most important reason for holding a potlatch was to mourn the death of a chief or solemnize the appointment of a new one. Winter dances engendered many potlatches, as each new dance title had to be officially witnessed. Life changes to close family were celebrated: a daughter's puberty, a son's new ceremonial name, or a marriage. The Bella Coola re-bought their wives: a father-in-law would pretend to take back his daughter, and her husband would be obliged to host a potlatch to re-buy her. The in-laws would help pay for the event, because

OPPOSITE **The Kwakiutl chief Mungo Martin once owned this ceremonial "copper" named "Great Killer Whale". The top piece was deliberately broken off at a 1942 potlatch to celebrate the initiation of his son into a dancing society. The bottom section was broken at a potlatch to respond to a rival chief's insult. The copper was thrown into the sea on the death of Chief Martin's brother. Recovered, it was displayed at the cradle ceremony for the chief's granddaughter. In 1960 Mungo Martin gave the copper to the Royal British Columbia Museum on the death of his son. (RBCM cn 9251, by permission of Peter and Mabel Knox)**

the re-buying potlatch meant prestige for both families. If a host lost face by spoiling a ritual or breaking a tribal rule, then he would hold a face-saving potlatch. The Tsimshian said that this was to "shut the mouth" of the guests; damage to honor had to be restored, and the guests were paid to witness it.

The planning and hosting of a potlatch was complex. It took years to save up enough wealth, and months to gather the necessary food. Invitations to neighboring tribes were sent out by a canoe party of high-ranking nobles, dancing on planks laid across two canoes. On the morning of the scheduled event the guests arrived, and were ushered into the main tribal house, where they sat in strict order according to rank. The host stood up before them; he wore in turn all the masks that he was entitled to wear, and displayed all his ceremonial privileges. The guests were thanked for watching this display, and large quantities of food were served. Guests would take home baskets of left-overs to redistribute amongst their own villagers.

After the feast came the gifts. A host spent months planning this, as he had to remember what each individual had given him at the last potlatch, and to make sure that he gave something better. After receiving their gifts the guests took their leave, and one of them usually issued a general invitation to a return potlatch sometime in the future. This guest went home and started accumulating goods for his turn.

This finely balanced system lost its equilibrium in the mid-19th century in Kwakiutl territory. In 1849 the Hudson's Bay Company set up Fort Rupert in the north of Vancouver Island to supervise a new coal mine. For the Kwakiutl, commerce in the region now centered on the fort rather than on the traditional trading places. Four tribes moved to Fort Rupert to take advantage of new activity, and formed a confederacy. Suddenly, there was an outsized tribe hosting potlatches of overwhelming abundance. With many more people to contribute property, and the availability of European goods from the Company post, the Fort Rupert potlatches created a form of runaway inflation in the system.

Intertribal warfare died out in the 1850s and 1860s, and the competitive potlatch became a substitute for actual raiding and fighting. It was an effective means of humbling an enemy tribe: two chiefs would see who could destroy, damage or throw away the most possessions. The chief who ruined the most property would prove himself to be the richer, and therefore the mightier. Canoes were burnt, slaves killed and valuable furs shredded. Most devastating of all, however, was the destruction of ceremonial "coppers". The copper was a shield that increased in value with age, as they were always sold at twice the price the vendor had paid. Coppers were bought and resold so many times that they acquired names and fame throughout the Coast. The burning or casting out to sea of a copper was an act of such sensational waste that it formed a "trump card" in the competitive potlatch. Eventually, one chief was forced to admit defeat, and the winner acquired for his tribe all the reflected glory of a military victory – although at ruinous cost.

The Canadian Indian Acts of 1885 and 1915 banned both the potlatch and the winter ceremonies. They carried on in secret for some time, but were hurt by the depression and the Pentecostal Church, who firmly banned the ceremony. The more moderate potlatch has had something of a rebirth since the 1960s and is thriving today.

WARFARE

War on the Coast

Raiding for slaves and booty was an integral part of life on the Northwest Coast, but when war proper was waged, it was done either to gain territory or to settle a feud. Both activities involved heavy loss of life, and became more lethal with the introduction of firearms.

The northern tribes of the Haida, Tsimshian and Tlingit were the most warlike. Haida canoes were said to have raided as far south as Cape Mendocino, California, and new research suggests that Kwakiutl canoe parties may also have raided that far south. A branch of the Kwakiutl, the Lekwiltok, were highly aggressive headhunters, raiding the other coastal peoples for their grim trophies. They also headhunted to honor their dead; as soon as one of their tribe died, a canoe party paddled to a neighboring village to kill someone of equal rank, or several people of inferior rank, in an act that was called "Let someone else wail."

The groups from mid-Vancouver Island southwards did not fight for purposes of expansion, but to redress wrongs. They carried intertribal feuds to bloody ends; these disputes were often many generations old, and led to a perpetual round of attack and counter-attack.

All the Coast tribes planned their tactics in elaborate detail. Usually the decision to go to war was made by all members of the tribe in one meeting. They discussed whether the reasons for war were just, and whether the village was strong enough to carry out such an attack. If necessary, the chief sent an envoy to a neighboring village to ask for extra help. The warriors then devised a plan of attack, using information from enemy captives already living amongst them as slaves. Maps of the target village were drawn in the sand, showing the exact sleeping quarters of the enemy chief, his nobles and fiercest warriors.

The villagers collected weapons, sharpened knives and prepared canoes. For a week prior to battle the young men bathed in the sea several times a day and scrubbed themselves with briars, to harden their skins against enemy weapons. While bathing, they chanted a prayer asking for bravery, strength, and the chance to kill as many of the enemy as possible.

The coastal warriors went to war heavily armed with bows and arrows, spears and pikes, which were not thrown but thrust. Clubs and daggers were carried for close fighting; the former were made of whalebone or stone and were called "slave killers". The northernmost tribes carried double-ended daggers held in the middle, which proved effective for upwards and downwards blows in hand-to-hand combat. Eventually the gun would replace the club and dagger in war, but bows and arrows took a long time to die out, since they were silent, quicker to reload, and often more accurate than early trade muskets. Warriors of the northern tribes wore carved and decorated wooden helmets, and protective armor of hide and bark (see Plate B for examples of these).

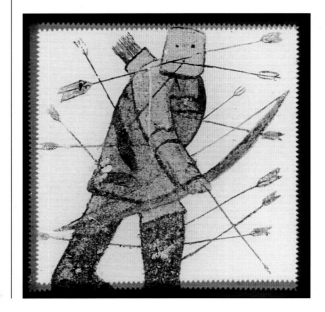

The artist Fred Alexcee lived at Fort Simpson in the 1880s. Using fish oils and glass, he painted scenes of Tsimshian life, including this warrior in body armor and helmet. (Vancouver Museum)

(continued on page 33)

THE NOOTKA POTLATCH
1: Chief Maquinna
2: Sat-Sat-Sok-Sis
3: Nootka woman

A

NORTHERN WARRIORS
1: Haida warrior
2: Tlingit warrior
3: Older Tlingit warrior

B

1: Weasel Dancer   3: Cannibal Dancer
2: Cannibal Bird Dancer   4: Warrior Dancer

SOUTHERN COASTAL TRIBES
1: Makah whaler
2: Cowichan warrior
3: Kwakiutl warrior
4: Coastal Salish warrior

D

THE DALLES
1: Wishram bride
2: Cayuse bridegroom

E

INTERIOR SALISH
1: Thompson River warrior
2: Thompson River woman
3: Flathead man

F

SAHAPTIN LANGUAGE TRIBES
1: Nez Perce warrior
2: Umatilla mother and baby
3: Umatilla chief

THE MODOC WAR, 1872–73
1: Kintpuash ("Captain Jack")
2: Modoc woman

H

War canoes were intended only for transport and not for battles at sea, although occasionally the enemy would try to board a canoe, and paddles were carved with sharp pointed tips so that they could double as weapons. A canoe carried from 20 to 40 men, and before an expedition was scorched and sanded along the bottom and sides to make it glide more smoothly through the water. The men shouted war songs as they paddled. Before landing close to an enemy village they arranged themselves in formation, and approached the shore in a silent and orderly fashion. Once at their destination, the men beached the canoes out of sight of the village and made their way individually towards the enemy.

Attacks usually took place at first light. If properly executed a raid could inflict a great deal of damage, but success depended on the element of surprise. This was not easy to achieve, since most villages posted sentinels, and night fishing expeditions meant someone was usually awake to raise the alarm. At this point, if something went wrong, the raiding party would run back to their canoes without hesitation. Archaeological evidence suggests that coastal villages were not easy to attack. They were heavily fortified with deep, wide ditches and a log stockade. According to oral history, the Tsimshian took defense one step further at the fort of Kitwanga, where they rolled whole tree trunks down the hill at attackers, with the branches sharpened to deadly points.

Once inside the village, most attacking warriors had pre-assigned victims. They made for the sleeping quarters and awaited the signal to attack, while their chief went directly to the house of his opposite number. When he seized the man's head, shrieked, and clubbed him to death, the other warriors followed his lead. In the ensuing confusion the attackers had the upper hand. The terrified residents, including women and children, would try to escape through secret exits in the plank walls, only to meet up with enemy warriors posted outside.

A battle between the Coast Salish Clallam and the Makah. Typically, war parties traveled by canoe to the vicinity of the target village in formation and landed in an orderly fashion. Once on shore, however, each warrior fought his way into the village on his own. Painting by Paul Kane. (The Royal Ontario Museum)

The victorious attackers dealt with the villagers in various ways. The old and infirm were killed, prisoners were taken as slaves, and the dead were decapitated and their heads taken to be displayed on poles. The victors carried home as many of the enemy's goods as possible, along with the slaves. Once back in the home village, the chief shared out the captured wealth. Those who had been especially brave were rewarded with a new name denoting their act.

War on the Plateau

Grievances between local tribes were often settled by making payments to the offended party. However, murder, harassment or abduction of a tribal woman demanded retaliation through war. Any territorial encroachment by an enemy tribe from the Plains or the Great Basin meant all-out war. The Klamath, Modoc and Molala fought primarily for economic reasons, since only by raiding and capturing slaves could they trade for horses and guns. The Modoc were the fiercest slavers, since they could not afford prolonged periods of peace.

The war chief would try to raise a war party, explaining all the reasons for war to the assembled tribe. The Nez Perce, Pend d'Oreille, and Flathead had their own versions of the Plains Crazy Dog warrior society, and would therefore have a group of professional warriors to draw upon. All other tribes had to recruit a fighting party afresh for each proposed war. Once the tribe had committed to action, a war dance was held to attract volunteers and stir up a warlike mood. In the Colville, Okanagan and Lakes region a warrior carried a blanket around the camp, and those wishing to fight would grasp it and sing. The newly recruited warriors now dressed up in their war clothes and performed a mock battle. Wasco Wishram warriors recounted dreams they had had about the coming confrontation, and affirmed how little they feared death.

To prepare themselves spiritually, warriors underwent a purifying sweat bath. For added support in battle some tribes took their shaman with them. He performed several tasks: prayed for success, cursed the enemy, fought alongside the warriors, and tended the wounded.

As the war party set out the village women sang, wishing them success and many scalps. While the war party was away they observed various rituals to keep their men safe. Occasionally women went along to help loot property or to guard any slaves taken.

The Plateau Indians rode to war with short bows and arrows well suited for shooting from horseback. The arrowheads were made of obsidian or stone, and many of the tribes dipped them in rattlesnake poison. Others made arrows with segmented heads that snapped off and stayed in the wound. They also carried a *pogamoggan*, which was a wooden truncheon-like weapon on one end of which was a bag containing a stone. As on the Coast, spears were used for stabbing rather than throwing.

Plateau armor consisted of a tunic of elk hide, sometimes of double thickness, which might also extend to the ankles. This made movement slow and awkward, so many preferred to fight without it, wearing only a breechcloth, moccasins and war charms. The Modoc stated that it was the duty of those not wearing armor to rush first into battle. Many painted their faces, the color varying from tribe to tribe. Most warriors painted their horses and bodies with the same color to show the union

A Tsimshian double-bladed dagger for hand-to-hand combat, usually made of trade metal. Before contact, the Coast probably obtained iron daggers through trade with Siberian tribes; an identical style of dagger is found in Siberia. (Royal British Columbia Museum cn 7220)

between man and horse. They would often draw tallies of those killed on their horses, chests or shirts. Salish chiefs went into battle in wolf headdresses with bear claws and trailing feathers, whereas other chiefs preferred the circlet of eagle feathers.

In a surprise attack, the enemy had to be located silently by the attackers; camp fires usually gave their position away. The war chief would send out scouts to discover where the chiefs and foremost warriors were housed within that camp. At first light the aggressors encircled the village, to rush in at a given signal. They formed an extended line, so the enemy had no main body of men to fire at. Once inside the village each man was on his own.

Not all battles started with a surprise attack. When two sides met for battle they would face each other for some while before attacking. Foot soldiers danced and yelled, and some of the horsemen gyrated in and out of their saddles. Gradually they advanced until they were some hundred yards apart; then the dancing stopped and the fighting began. The younger, swifter riders would be placed at the front of the lines. Some warriors believed themselves protected from arrows or bullets by their guardian spirit, and would ride out first to draw the enemy fire. Foot soldiers leapt from side to side to dodge arrows; other warriors rode hanging down one side of their horse, so the enemy believed that riderless horses were coming towards them. Nez Perce members of the Crazy Dog Society took up positions in the thick of the combat, and drove a stake into the ground pinning the end of a sash;

Nootka fisherman, photographed by Edward S.Curtis. Simple wooden bows were used for hunting and fishing, but for war compound bows were carried, strengthened with sinew and glued with pitch. The Coast tribes made arrows from red cedar, but the Plateau peoples preferred harder woods such as yew and juniper; these were difficult to break off, and caused more bleeding. (Royal British Columbia Museum pn 4856)

they were sworn not to move from that spot until someone relieved them or the fight ended. Battles were brief but intense. Some tribes, such as the Wasco Wishram, refused to fight at night. If the encounter dragged on longer than daylight, each side would retire to their camp to spend the night hurling insults at the other, and fighting would resume at first light.

One side would eventually dominate the other. The defeated side retreated or sent an envoy to the opposing chief asking for a parley. In small intertribal wars, each side would tally up how many were dead, and pay compensation to the other for those killed; they paid nothing for captives taken. In larger conflicts, the immediate aftermath was bloody. The retreating side was forced to leave its dead and seriously injured on the field, while the victors took booty and scalps. Scalping was an act of humiliation, as the Indians believed it affected their spirit life. Some tribes mutilated the bodies of their victims, depending on the bitterness of the conflict. Enemy corpses were often burnt, and the surrounding area searched for hidden women and children. Injured enemy were killed with poisoned arrows. The Modoc, Klamath and Molala were not

Brodeck Indian stockade, Noonyah village – note the totem heads. The northernmost tribes all used fortified villages at the time of contact with the white man. The palisade has two entrances with two different types of steps: those at left are conventional, but that just visible in the center has the traditional notched log ladder that could be pulled inside in case of enemy attack. The equally sloped props holding up the wall may have been used for rolling logs down on to attackers. (Canadian Museum of Civilization. Negative no.78-6041)

so interested in scalps as they were in slaves. Instead of each warrior proudly displaying the number of scalps he had taken, they entrusted the entire war party's enemy scalps to one man who carried them home, thus freeing the warriors to deal with their slaves.

When the victorious war party returned to its village there was a scalp or victory dance. These usually consisted of the villagers dancing in a circle with the enemy scalps held high on poles. Captive enemies were humiliated, and made to stand in the center of the circle while the dancers threw insults and blows at them. Widows of dead warriors were given first turn at this abuse. Brave warriors recited their deeds and feasted, before going to the sweathouse to be purified.

AMERICAN INDIAN WARS

The Tlingit put up fierce resistance to the Russians in the first two decades of the 19th century. In 1802, Chief Katlian captured the Russian fort of New Archangel (Sitka) and held it for two years. He and his followers were driven out by a force of 120 Russians and 1,000 Aleut headed by Alexander Baranov, the chief manager of the Russian American Company. From this point, the Tlingit continued to attack trading posts and harass traders. The Russians maintained a fragile order using gunboats, but never completely settled the problem. After the US Alaska purchase in 1867, the Tlingit used the same tactics on the Americans, until disease and depopulation finally weakened them.

The rest of the Coast and Plateau enjoyed a relatively peaceful period between first contact and the 1840s. Then the Oregon Trail opened, and streams of settlers poured in looking for land. The US government recognized the need to protect native property and rights, but came under pressure from the settlers to disregard Indian claims to territory. The 1846 Organic Act affirmed that Indians could not lose lands without consent. It was followed two years later by the Oregon Donation

A Flathead dance performed on the Montana reservation, c1905. The dancers are wearing typical war dress for the Interior Salish: a breechcloth, moccasins and a simple head band, although some display hair roach headdresses. (Denver Public Library, Western History Collection. Edward Boos BS121)

Act, granting 320 free acres to any settler in Oregon over the age of 18 years; settlers and Indians were now in direct conflict over land.

The Cayuse War, 1847

The first clash occurred at a Presbyterian mission at Waiilatpu in Cayuse territory. Relations between the Cayuse and the minister, Marcus Whitman, had always been uneasy, and when a measles epidemic broke out the Indians blamed the mission. Two warriors killed the Reverend Whitman with a tomahawk, shot his wife and took 50 others hostage. The local settlers raised a volunteer militia, which attacked several native villages in the area, killing innocent Indians in reprisal. Other Plateau Basin tribes threatened to join the Cayuse. The hostages were rescued, the situation eventually calmed down, and the culprits were tried and hanged. After this the Americans set up more military posts in the area, and established a territorial government to help the newcomers settle in.

The Yakima War, 1855–56

In 1855 Governor Isaac Stevens held the Walla Walla Council to make treaties with the tribes in Washington Territory. He asked them to relinquish their lands in return for reservations, education, cattle, horses and money. Most importantly to the Indians at the council, Stevens promised that they could stay on their lands for a couple of years after the treaty was ratified. The majority signed the agreement, even though many wanted to hold out for better terms. Twelve days later, Stevens declared native lands open for white settlers. The Indians prepared for war.

Chief Kamiakin emerged as the leader of the dissidents; half-Nez Perce, half-Yakima, he was called by the whites "The Sullen Chief". He tried to form an alliance of all the Columbia Basin tribes to go to war, but before he had time to pull them together his nephew, Qualchin, killed six miners and the Indian Agent who came to investigate their deaths, and the war had begun.

A force of 500 soldiers left Fort Dalles under Maj Granville O'Haller. They were met by Kamiakin and a combined force of Yakima, Cayuse, Umatilla, Walla Walla and Palouse; the warriors defeated the US force, although only five soldiers were killed. Several skirmishes between the two groups followed, and a volunteer militia formed by local settlers joined in.

The US Army had little control over these volunteers, who sometimes acted brutally. When Chief Peopeomoxmox of the Walla Walla came under a white flag to parley with the militia he was killed, and his scalp and ears were put on display. As the situation deteriorated the militia killed innocent Indians, and some Army officers began to favor a policy of aboriginal extermination.

There was no distinct end to the conflict. In April and May the authorities sent out "friendly" Indians to scout down the "criminals"; these wore blue caps trimmed with red, made by the ladies of Olympia to tell them apart from Kamiakin's men. By early summer many of the dissidents had fled east, and the war wound down, waiting to flare up again in the future.

The Nisqually War, 1855–56

Governor Stevens' plan to place several tribes together in every reservation often meant Indians were forced into unfamiliar environments. The Nisqually (Coast Salish) were moved from their tribal grasslands into a forested reservation. Chief Leschi of the Nisqually

May 18, 1855: the Walla Walla Council, which began the treaty process between US authorities and the Columbia Basin tribes. At center, Governor Isaac Stevens and his party wait beneath the flagpole, among hundreds of painted Nez Perce riders. It would be 22 years before the government's reneging on the agreement drove the Nez Perce into hopeless war; for the Yakima it would only take 12 days for Stevens to go back on his word. Drawing by Gustavus Sohon. (National Anthropological Archives, Smithsonian Institute INV 08602800)

decided to fight; he planned to attack the settlers, and contacted the Yakima and other tribes to join him. Chief Seattle of the Salish refused to support the malcontents, and dissuaded other tribes from joining. In January 1856, Leschi's combined forces attacked the settlement of Seattle, but one of his nephews had betrayed him to the authorities. The US gunboat *Decatur* was waiting for them, and bombarded the tribal force from Puget Sound. Many were killed and the remaining warriors scattered. Chief Leschi was captured, tried and hanged.

The Coeur d'Alene War, 1858

This is sometimes called the Second Yakima War because it involved the same combination of tribes as the 1855 war, plus warriors from the Coeur d'Alene, Spokane and Northern Paiute. This was the last time the Columbia Basin tribes combined against the whites. Increased mining activity in the Columbia Valley, and unsatisfactory treaties with the whites, had stirred up former antagonisms. Chief Kamiakin once again called for the Basin tribes to form an alliance.

In May 1858 a small column of 164 US soldiers – three companies of the 1st Dragoons and 25 infantry manning two mountain howitzers, under Maj Edward Steptoe – left Fort Walla Walla and entered Kamiakin's territory. On May 17, near Tohatonimme Creek, they were attacked by some 1,000 Indians. They reached a hilltop and defended themselves, and when down to three rounds per man they buried the guns and slipped away by night, having suffered six dead and twelve

This Nisqually man, Wahoolit, fought alongside Chief Leschi in the 1855–56 Puget Sound war, and in the famous attack on Fort Seattle. He killed Sluggia, Leschi's treacherous nephew, and was sentenced to hang for it, only to be pardoned on the day of his execution. It is not clear if the skull on the table belonged to Sluggia. (University of Washington Libraries, Special Collections Division NA 1358)

wounded. Brimming with confidence from this encounter, Kamiakin's men then confronted a force of 600 troops – four companies of the 1st Dragoons and six of infantry – at Four Lakes on September 1. The infantry and two howitzers drove them out of a rocky, wooded ravine and into open country where the dragoons rode them down, killing about 60 for no loss. On September 5, Capt William Grier's troopers repeated this success at Spokan Plain. The Indians lost heart and their alliance crumbled; warriors dispersed to their respective villages, where the Army later arrested many of them. Kamiakin escaped to Canada.

The Modoc War, 1872–73

The American Civil War put an end to the treaty process, and with most regular troops fighting in the East, Indian control was left in the hands of volunteer forces. During the war and its aftermath any Indian risings were dealt with summarily by these often poorly disciplined troops, and – as in the case of the Modoc and the Nez Perce – would flare up again before long.

The materially poor Modoc came from the Tule Lake region of southern Oregon and northern California. By the 1860s local settlers in the area were complaining of them stealing cattle, selling

Kintpuash or "Captain Jack", leader of the Modoc dissidents. Unable to steer his followers in the moderate direction he wished, against the influence of the shaman Curly Haired Doctor, he led them in a brave but hopeless rebellion. This photograph was taken by Louis Herman Heller on the day of Jack's capture, June 1 1873. He was executed on October 3 for murdering Gen Edward R.S.Canby during peace talks. (National Anthropological Archives, Smithsonian Institute INV 01604204)

their women to miners, and continually fighting, and demanded that the tribe be moved to a reservation. In 1864, under pressure from the authorities, the Modoc reluctantly signed an agreement to live on a reservation with their old rivals the Klamath. After they had settled in a group of Paiute – the Modoc's deadliest enemies – were also moved to the same reservation.

Chief Kintpuash, known as "Captain Jack" to the whites, left the Klamath Reservation with a small group of followers and returned to the Tule Lake area. The settlers protested, and over the next five years the authorities tried everything to persuade Captain Jack and his splinter group back to the reservation, while a steady stream of other Modoc left it and joined his band. He demanded a separate Modoc reservation at Lost River, but was refused. Jack was a moderate, but in his camp was a powerful shaman called Curly Haired Doctor, who followed the Ghost Dance religion. This was a militant sect who believed, among other articles of faith, that all Indians who were killed would be resurrected; since they did not fear death, the Ghost Dancers urged violent resistance to all whites. Curly Haired Doctor and his group pushed Captain Jack into a more militant position.

In November 1872 a force of troops tried to drive the rebel Modoc back to the reservation; one man on each side was killed. The Modoc then fled to the Lava Beds, an almost impassable area of jagged volcanic rock. A group led by one Hooker Jim killed 15 settlers; the Army called in reinforcements, and followed the Modoc to their refuge, where Captain Jack set up camp in a cavern. Curly Haired Doctor protected it by stringing around the perimeter a red tule rope which he claimed that whites could not cross, setting up a medicine flag, and leading ritual dances. These ceremonies stiffened the morale of the fugitives, who numbered only 51.

Troops under Col Frank Wheaton brought Jack's stronghold under fire in January 1873, but the cover afforded by the volcanic terrain seemed impregnable; the Modoc counter-attacked, killed several soldiers and forcing others to retreat, leaving behind them abandoned rifles and ammunition. Curly Haired Doctor grew more powerful after this incident, since the troops had killed no Indians and no white man had crossed the red rope.

The military commander of the Northwest, BrigGen Edward Canby, brought in more troops, and opened peace negotiations in a tent erected between the two camps. Captain Jack asked for a Modoc reservation in the Lava Beds, and refused to surrender Hooker Jim for the murder of the Tule Lake ranchers. Negotiations stalled, and the militants in the Modoc camp grew angry at news that the Army had enlisted Indian scouts from the Warm Springs tribe on the Columbia River. Completely misunderstanding white psychology, Hooker Jim and Curly Haired Doctor urged Captain Jack that if Canby were killed the enemy would crumble. On April 11, in the "peace tent", Captain Jack pulled a hidden revolver and killed Canby, while another Modoc, Boston Charley, killed the peace commissioner, the Rev Eleasar Thomas.

When the soldiers renewed their attacks the Modoc retreated to a lava plateau to the south. On April 26 a group of Modoc attacked a force of 80 troops trying to install a howitzer on a volcanic butte, killing 22 including the five officers. Short of food and water, however, the Modoc now scattered into small groups; and with the help of the Warm Springs scouts the Army was able to kill or capture them group by group. When Hooker Jim surrendered the Army persuaded him to help track down Captain Jack, who was captured on June 1. The rebellion was over; and at Jack's trial his own men – particularly Hooker Jim – testified as witnesses against him. He was found guilty and hanged. Some accounts claim that his body was subsequently dug up, embalmed, and put on display at eastern carnivals.

The Nez Perce War, 1877

At the 1855 Walla Walla Council, the Nez Perce agreed to sign the treaty provided that they could stay in their ancestral home of the Wallowa Valley. The US government agreed; but the 1860s gold rush in the area changed their minds. A new treaty was proposed: the Nez Perce reservation was reduced from 100,000 square miles to 1,000 square miles, none of which were in the Wallowa Valley. The tribe was split; Chief Lawyer wanted peace and signed the treaty, but Chief Old Joseph and his followers refused, and moved quietly back to the Wallowa Valley, where they stayed for the next few years. After the death of Old Joseph in 1873, his sons Ollikut and Young Joseph faced a new wave of settlers in the valley, many of whom arrived on the brand new railroad. President Grant tried to enforce the Wallowa Valley as a Nez Perce reservation, but the ranchers and miners ignored this ruling.

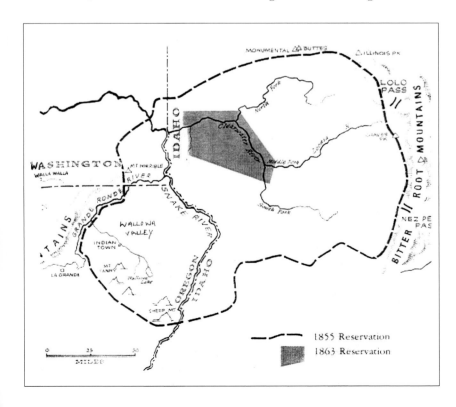

Map showing the 100,000 square mile Nez Perce Reservation as proposed in 1855. The shaded patch is the 1,000 square mile Lapwaii Reservation onto which the tribe was forced in 1863. (Based on the Lucullus McWhorter map)

In May 1877, under pressure from the settlers, the government ordered the Nez Perce back to their 1863 reservation at Lapwaii. General Oliver Howard gave them 30 days to comply, or refusal would constitute an act of war. While Joseph and his moderates discussed the situation, militants killed 20 settlers. General Howard prepared to arrest them; Joseph and Ollikut decided to support their militant brothers, and to leave the area immediately. This was the beginning of a three-month, 1,300-mile flight.

The first action of the Nez Perce War took place on the morning of June 11, when a troop of some 99 cavalry under Capt David Perry attacked a camp at White Bird Canyon. The Indians were caught by surprise, and many of them were unwell, having captured a whisky barrel the day before; in spite of this they killed 34 soldiers without losing a man. (The Nez Perce were excellent marksmen, despite their motley collection of firearms; the US Army of the 1870s was notorious for the lack of live firing training that the soldiers received.) At this point another group of dissidents from the Nez Perce reservation joined Chief Joseph, bringing the strength of the group to about 700 – but of these, some 550 were women, children and old people.

The US Army employed Bannock scouts, whose skills enabled Gen Howard to stay on the fugitives' trail through the most difficult conditions. His troops attacked the Nez Perce again at the Clearwater River, where warriors fought the troops for two days while the rest of the tribe escaped; 13 soldiers died, and four Nez Perce. The group now decided to turn east and ask help from their allies the Crow; Howard lost track of them at this point, but he wired ahead to Army posts in the Missoula region ordering them to intercept the Nez Perce. Volunteer militia erected a barricade to stop the Indians in a pass across the Rockies. The Nez Perce met the volunteers for a brief parley; and after each side had refused the other's demands, the Nez Perce simply climbed around the barricade and traveled on (the site was afterwards known as "Fort Fizzle"). Comic as the incident was, it also brought the fleeing Indians bitter news: their former allies, the Flathead, were helping the militia. On a more positive note, the fugitives and the ranchers of the Bitterroot Valley agreed that the Nez Perce would pass through their territory in peace.

On August 9, some 200 troops and volunteers under Col John Gibbon attacked the Nez Perce camp at Big Hole Valley; swooping in at first light, they killed 89 Nez Perce – 77 of whom were women and children, but also including some of their

A group of thin, exhausted Nez Perce after their surrender in Montana, and before they were taken to Oklahoma. (Northwest Museum of Arts and Culture/Eastern Washington State Historical Society, Spokane, Washington, L94-7.148)

best warriors, among them Joseph's brother Ollikut. After the initial surprise the warriors rallied and drove off their attackers – among whom they recognized ranchers from the Bitterroot Valley who had promised to let them pass in peace. It was a turning point in the whole campaign; the Nez Perce lost most of their possessions at Big Hole Valley, and would never trust any white man again. As they continued their flight eastwards they attacked any settlers they met.

On August 19 the Nez Perce raided Gen Howard's camp at Camas Meadows and drove off the Army pack mules; while the soldiers rounded them up, the Indians headed for Wyoming. They cut through the newly formed Yellowstone Park, where they terrified visiting naturalists and tourists, and made their way towards Crow territory in Montana. The Crow, however, refused to help them; this was another hard blow, made worse when they learnt that Crow were scouting for the Army. The chiefs decided to travel north to Canada and shelter at Sitting Bull's camp among the Sioux.

They traveled through the most difficult terrain, where the Army could not follow; but once again, Gen Howard had wired ahead, and 360 men under Capt Sturgis from Fort Keogh in Montana caught up with the band as they passed through Canyon Creek. Once more, the warriors kept up a delaying fire on the oncoming troops while the rest of the tribe escaped; then they blocked the canyon with brush and rocks, and followed.

On September 23 the Nez Perce, now very short on supplies, raided an Army depot at Cow Island on the Missouri River crossing. They successfully fought off a contingent of soldiers from Fort Benton, but by now the band were exhausted. Chief Looking Glass took command as they headed towards Canada; Gen Howard had again lagged behind, but wired Col Nelson Miles to cut across from Fort Keogh. On September 30 the Nez Perce were camped and resting at Bear Paw Pass, confident that they had evaded Howard's pursuit when, just as they were preparing to move off, Col Miles attacked, helped by Cheyenne scouts. Some of the group escaped north into Canada while the rest fought to hold the soldiers off. Among the heavy Indian casualties 25 were killed and many wounded. Colonel Miles also lost numbers of men, but his troops surrounded the Nez Perce camp. Peace talks between Chief Joseph and Col Miles were attempted but soon abandoned; the two forces settled into a stalemate punctuated by exchanges of fire.

On October 4, Gen Howard and his column finally came up; Chief Joseph realized that the position was irretrievable, and surrendered. The last casualty of the war was Chief Looking Glass, who was shot when he stood up after mistaking a party of Col Miles' Cheyenne scouts for a rescue party of Sioux from Canada. Chief Joseph's speech of surrender summed up the tribe's exhaustion and despair. He and his people were taken to Oklahoma; they eventually lived out their days on the Lapwaii Reservation, Idaho, and the Colville Reservation in Washington State.

On October 5, 1877, Chief Joseph of the Nez Perce finally surrendered to the US Army: "It is cold and we have no blankets. The little children are freezing to death. My people, some of them, have run away to the hills, and have no blankets, no food. No one knows where they are – perhaps freezing to death. I want to have time to look for my children and see how many I can find. Maybe I shall find them among the dead. Hear me, my chiefs. I am tired. My heart is sick and sad. From where the sun now stands, I will fight no more forever." This 1897 photograph is by M.Sawyer Wells. (University of Washington Libraries, Special Collections Division. NA 879)

SELECT BIBLIOGRAPHY

Boas, Franz, *Bella Bella Texts* (New York, 1928)
Boyd, Robert, *The People of The Dalles* (Bloomington, c1996)
Curtis, Edward S., *Curtis' Western Indians* (New York, 1962)
Duff, Wilson, *Impact of the White Man* (Victoria, 1965)
Drucker, Philip, *Cultures of the North Pacific Coast* (San Francisco, 1965)
Fahey, John, *Flathead Indians* (Oklahoma, 1974)
Holm, Bill, *Box of Daylight: Northwest Coast Indian Art* (Seattle, 1983)
Holm, Bill, *Indian Art of the Northwest Coast* (Vancouver, BC, 1975)
Jewitt, John, *The Adventures and Sufferings of John R. Jewitt: captive of Maquinna* (Vancouver, BC, 1987)
Lillard, Charles, *Nootka – Scenes and Studies of Savage Life, Gilbert Malcolm Sproat* (Victoria, BC, 1987)
Lewis, Meriwether, *The History of the Expedition of Captains Lewis and Clark, 1804–5* (Chicago, 1902)
MacDonald, George F., *Kitwanga Fort Report* (Ottawa, 1976)
MacDonald, George F., *The Dig: an Archaeological Reconstruction of a West Coast Village* (Hull, Quebec, 1989)
McIlwraith, T.F., *The Bella Coola Indians* (Toronto, 1992)
McWhorter, Lucullus Virgil, *Hear me, My Chiefs* (Caldwell, Idaho, 1983)
Moziño, José Mariano, *Noticias de Nootka: an Account of Nootka Sound, 1792* (Seattle, 1991)
Murray, Keith A., *The Modocs and Their War* (Norman, Oklahoma, 1959)
Nuytten, Phil, 'Money From the Sea', *National Geographic* (January 1993)
Ray, Verne F., *Primitive Pragmatists; The Modoc Indians of Northern California* (Seattle, 1963)
Ruby, Robert A., & John A. Brown, *Indians of the Pacific Northwest: a History* (Norman, Oklahoma, 1981)
Smithsonian Institution, *Handbook of North American Indians Vol. 7 – The Northwest Coast* (Washington, 1978)
Smithsonian Institution, *Handbook of North American Indians Vol. 12 – The Plateau* (Washington, 1978)
Swanton, J.R., *The Indian Tribes of North America* (Washington, 1953)
Teit, James H., *The Thompson Indians of British Columbia* (New York, 1975)
Waldman, Carl, *The Atlas of North American Indians* (New York, 2000)
Woodcock, George, *British Columbia, A History of the Province* (Vancouver, 1990)

THE PLATES

A: THE NOOTKA POTLATCH

In 1802 a handful of Nootka Indians under Chief Maquinna overran the US trading ship *Boston* and killed almost the entire crew. They spared only the blacksmith John Jewitt and his friend John Thompson, holding them as slaves for two years. After taking the ship Maquinna held a potlatch, the traditional northwest ceremony held to mark important events. He invited neighboring villages to attend a feast and to receive goods taken from the ship.

A1: Chief Maquinna

As the host of the potlatch he is the most important person present. He wears a sea-otter robe, which only nobility are allowed to wear. His hair is greased and sprinkled with eagle down, which was believed to bring luck. (Down has also been sprinkled around the room before the dance.) He wears large mother-of-pearl earrings and several bracelets made of trade iron. In each hand he waves a trade musket from the pile of looted guns behind him.

A2: Sat-Sat-Sok-Sis

Maquinna's son performs a Wolf Dance – usually part of the winter ceremonies, but also danced at potlatches. He is wrapped in trade cloth, possibly from the ship. The wolf mask is made of wood with cedar bark trimmings. He wears a shredded cedar-bark skirt, and carries a wooden rattle.

A3: Nootka woman

The woman wears a cape and robe of cedar bark edged with sea-otter fur, and a painted basketry hat, decorated with beads.

B: NORTHERN WARRIORS

The fiercest warriors came from the northern tribes – the Tlingit, Haida and Tsimshian – who raided far down the coast. Behind these three figures note a Haida war canoe pulled up on the beach; based upon an example exhibited in the Canadian Museum of Civilization, it is 54ft (16.5m) long, holds a crew of ten and could carry three sails.

B1: Haida warrior

The Haida divide themselves into two groups, the Raven and the Eagle; each group inherits certain crests and privileges. This warrior is from the Eagle clan, and has the associated crests of eagle and killer whale on his hide armor and tattooed on his shoulder. His helmet is a grotesque head with added human hair and a set of teeth, and he wears Tsimshian leather leggings that tie behind the legs. He carries a knife of trade metal, and a wooden club.

B2: Tlingit warrior
Wooden helmets were carved in the shape of mythical monsters. The Tlingit chose gnarled and knotted pieces of wood that would not crack easily when hit. This one, with inlaid copper "eyebrows", comes from the Múseo de América in Madrid. Below this, the warrior wears a wooden face guard with a small ventilation hole; he peers out below the helmet through two small cut-outs in the upper rim of the face guard. The Tlingit's traditional moose-hide armor proved ineffective when the Russians arrived in Alaska, but adding Chinese trade coins made the armor to some degree bulletproof. The warrior carries a trade gun.

B3: Older Tlingit warrior
This warrior wears two thicknesses of caribou hide, beneath cedar-slat armor hinged with leather and fastened at the shoulders with wooden toggles; it is painted with motifs on chest and belly. He carries a double-bladed dagger, of which the shorter upper blade could be used to stab upwards in close combat, and a stone and wood club known as a "slave killer".

C: DANCE CEREMONIES
These usually took place in winter, and were performed by members of a secret dance society. The Kwakiutl and Bella Coola were adept at stagecraft; and since the dances took place indoors by the light of one central fire, they were able to use the articulated masks and noise-makers to dramatic effect.

C1: Weasel Dancer
This dance takes place in summer. The dancer wears an elaborate hawk headdress of swan's down, the frontal plaque of wood with abalone inlay, and the rear train of ermine skins; a circlet of baleen whiskers on top of the headdress is filled with eagle down, which is scattered as the dancer bobs up and down. Below the red and black button blanket, his dance apron has rattles of puffin bills and thimbles. A tasseled collar of cedar bark is worn around the neck, and he carries a wooden raven rattle. He bobs up and down, with his feet close together and his elbows stuck out, and the other dancers ridicule him for his awkward dance; he disappears to the spirit world, then reappears after a short interval transformed into a mythical being.

C2: Cannibal Bird Dancer
This Kwakiutl figure attends the Cannibal Dancer. The wooden articulated mask snaps open and shut, and is

Tlingit war helmet; see Plate B. The helmet would be placed on top of a wooden faceguard with eye cut-outs in its upper edge, and would give the warrior several extra inches of height. About 4ins thick, these wooden helmets afforded considerable protection. (Peabody Museum, Harvard University. T2074)

supposed to crack open human skulls. The dancer wears an enveloping cape/skirt of shredded cedar bark.

C3: Cannibal Dancer
The dancer is carried off to the upper world by the Cannibal Spirit, and comes back eating nothing but human flesh. He bites the audience (although this is prearranged, and later paid off in gifts called "bandages"). The dance tames him, and he returns to normal. This Bella Coola dancer wears a trade blanket with carved wooden skulls and cedar-bark tassels attached. The substantial cedar-bark collar is to tether him when he turns wild. He carries a hidden whistle to make sound effects that the villagers believe come from the spirits. His hair is short – it has been blown off in the Upper World.

C4: Warrior Dancer
This Kwakiutl woman performs the Warrior Dance, during which she is beheaded in gory and convincing detail; after a few hours' absence she comes back to life. The dance society carvers have fashioned a wooden head in her image to make the beheading believable.

D: SOUTHERN COASTAL TRIBES
D1: Makah whaler
He wears a bearskin robe and a basketwork hat decorated with whaling motifs. Tied to his heavy harpoon are floats made from inflated seal bladders. Just visible below his left hand is a bone rattle; once a whale has been harpooned the whaler will use the rattle, together with traditional chants, to turn the whale towards the beach.

D2: Cowichan warrior
Black paint is applied to his face and legs. He wears a thick buckskin shirt as protection in battle, decorated with attached eagle feathers; it shows slits from previous fights. A walrus-tusk war club is stuck into his plaited cedar-bark belt, but his main weapon is a spear used for thrusting rather than throwing; note its split shaft tied with bark strips, and the bunch of eagle feathers partially hiding its stone tip.

D3: Kwakiutl warrior
The Kwakiutl were fierce headhunters, and greatly feared along the southern coast. This warrior, his face blackened with charcoal, has tied his hair up with bark strips to make it harder for an enemy to grab it in combat. He wears an armor of coiled rope above a cedar-bark kilt. His weapons are a knife of trade metal with a bone handle, and a war club carved in the shape of a killer whale with a dorsal fin made of stone.

D4: Coast Salish warrior
Before going off to war, this man tries to make his canoe glide more smoothly through the water. He has scorched the underside with burning cedar twigs or hemlock branches; now he sands it, using a piece of rough dogfish skin wrapped around a stone.

E: THE DALLES

The narrowing of the Columbia River produces a series of waterfalls and stretches of white water. The area became an important trade and fishing center, with white trade goods, especially guns, coming directly from the coast. The Nez Perce and Cayuse kept tribesmen permanently encamped at the Dalles to ensure they secured a major share of the arms passing through. Many intertribal alliances and marriages also took place there; in the foreground are a bridal couple, and baskets full of fruit.

E1: Wishram bride
This young woman of about 16 years wears a long hanging veil made of dentalium shells, beads and Chinese coins, with a necklace and ear drops; another dentalium shell pierces her nasal septum. Her elaborately beaded Plateau dress, based on dark blue trade cloth, is largely hidden here by the elk hide which is wrapped around her and her groom to symbolize their union. It too is decorated with a lavishly beaded strip of blanket cloth; the symbol of the hourglass represents a woman, the rectangular shape, a man, and the rosette is the circle of life.

E2: Cayuse bridegroom
A man of about 20, he too wears a necklace and ear ornaments, and a richly painted and beaded buckskin shirt. Across his chest from his right shoulder a bandolier bag is partly visible; the beadwork strap has red "bear-claw" marks, symbolizing the wounds suffered by a famous Cayuse warrior at the hands of a grizzly bear.

(Background) Salmon are plentiful and easy to catch in the falls. Fishermen stood on wooden platforms built out over the water, and used large nets or double-pointed spears.

F: INTERIOR SALISH

The Salish-speaking tribes live in the central part of the Plateau in mountainous surroundings and extreme temperatures.

F1: Thompson River warrior
He wears his hair with a feather sticking upright on the brow, in a style borrowed from the Plains Indians. Under his painted buckskin cape he sports a traditional bandolier bag, complete with intricate beadwork, bells and Hudson's Bay Company buttons. Buckskin leggings with multiple fringes, and moccasins with floral beadwork motifs, complete his clothing. He carries a short Thompson River bow and a small wooden war club covered with hide strips on a hide wrist loop.

F2: Thompson River woman
Her deerskin cap is decorated with beadwork and Hudson's Bay Company buttons. Her fur and buckskin cape is displayed in the Canadian Museum of Civilization; the design on the buckskin rosette symbolizes the sun. Her leggings show a traditional pattern in black and white beads; and she plays a hide drum.

F3: Flathead man
This older man wears a traditional animal-hair roach headdress with trailing ermine tails. His coat is made from a Hudson's Bay blanket. He wears a slung tobacco pouch and carries a beaded knife sheath on its strap. He is smoking a carved soapstone pipe.

G: SAHAPTIN LANGUAGE TRIBES

These live in the southern Plateau region, along the Columbia River and its tributaries. Their clothes, houses and

A Bella Bella articulated mask as used in Coast winter ceremonies; see Plate C. The mechanism allowed the performer to act out the roles of two different characters, or to demonstrate the transformation of one creature into another. (Royal British Columbia Museum cn 11)

way of life show a marked Plains influence. Many of the beaded articles in this plate are based on artifacts in the Doris Swayze Bounds Collection, in the High Desert Museum.

G1: Nez Perce warrior
He rides an Appaloosa – these were the sturdiest and most valuable horses on the Plateau. Both horse and rider have been painted for war, with streaks of red, yellow and blue; note also that the horse's mane is dyed black and its tail red. The warrior has a bead choker and a loop necklace; he wears a split-horn bonnet with a beaded headband and dangling ermine tails, and a bell strung between the horns. His buckskin shirt is decorated with quillwork; his trade blanket leggings obscure here the high, unbeaded ankles of his moccasins. A bandolier bag and its long, broad red cloth strap are decorated with beadwork. He carries an 1866 Winchester carbine.

A Haida carving of argillite, a soft, fine-grained shale found in one quarry in the Queen Charlotte Islands. The Haida began carving pipes covered in crests and crest figures for funeral rituals, which sailors from trading vessels took home as souvenirs. This carving is about 20in high. (Canadian Museum of Civilization, image S95-03983)

G2: Umatilla mother and baby
This young woman's beaded dress is made of two deerskins sewn together, with a tail left on display in front just below the neckline. Her corn-husk bag and basketry hat show traditional geometric patterns, later discouraged by missionaries and replaced with floral designs. The baby is strapped to a buckskin cradleboard with a beaded headboard.

G3: Umatilla chief
He wears an eagle feather circlet headdress. His buckskin shirt and leggings are decorated with black and white pony beads, and are worn with a fringed breechcloth of tartan. He wears a beaded necklace with bear claws set at intervals, and holds a ceremonial buffalo-fur stick.

H: THE MODOC WAR, 1872–73
H1: Kintpuash ("Captain Jack")
With his face painted white, he sits in the cave known as the "Stronghold", playing a hide drum laced over a rectangular frame as part of a Ghost Dance ritual to protect his followers from the soldiers' bullets. He is dressed in ordinary white workmen's clothes of a striped calico shirt and old blue trousers; he was photographed in a white cap which may have been formed by cutting off all except the front brim of a shallow-crowned hat. Strips of hide have been wound around his hands to allow him to clamber safely over the jagged lava rocks. Beside him lies a Springfield rifle captured from the US troops.

H2: Modoc woman
Women and children remained in the Stronghold throughout the campaign. This woman's clothing is a mix of traditional Modoc and 19th century trade clothes.

TOP **These finely beaded Thompson River armbands would be used for ceremonial purposes. Buckskin clothing was whitened with clay before the beads were applied. See Plate F. (Canadian Museum of Civilization II-C-392 ab, image no.75-13359)**

ABOVE **Haida moccasins, beaded on the vamp and lined with fur. Most Coast tribes preferred to go shoeless, but had elaborate beaded moccasins for ceremonial purposes. (Canadian Museum of Civilization VII-B-1178a-b, image no.S96-005685)**

Her blue print calico dress and tartan blanket are trade items, her basketwork hat is traditional Modoc; a necklace of pine nuts would also be typical. She sits by the "medicine flag" made of hawk feathers and weasel skin hanging from a stick. The clearing in the cave is encircled with a red rope cordon that the shaman promises will keep white men out.

(Background) A US Army scout, recruited from the Warm Springs people on the Columbia river, creeps closer. They appear to have been issued 1858 pattern Hardee hats and four-button blue "sack" coats, and a photograph shows civilian cord or "ticken" trousers and Army shoes. Their weapon was the Spencer repeating rifle.

INDEX